Most people want to see enhanced trade and we increasingly like to travel there. Wha part of a state called Europe, which determin daily lives. We don't want our laws decided l want unlimited immigration and nor do we wish to be obliged to pay the ever increasing bill of EU membership. We want to govern ourselves.

Britain faces an increasingly uncertain future in a rapidly changing world and our membership of the EU is hindering, not helping, Britain's response. The EU is simply not up to the task of addressing the competitive challenge from China, India, Brazil and other emerging economic power houses. The EU has woefully let down both British farmers as well as struggling nations in the Third World with its adherence to the Common Agricultural Policy. The EU's Schengen arrangements ensure the free flow of illegal migrants through much of the EU all the way up to Britain's borders.

When Britain voted in 1975 to remain a member of the Common Market, the arguments then were all about the importance of free trade. However, as 'A House Divided' makes clear, since then the Common Market has mutated into the European Economic Community (EEC), then the European Community (EC) and then the European Union (EU) all without any subsequent referendum. You now have to be 53 years of age to have been eligible to have taken part in the 1975 referendum and so there are millions of British people who have never had a specific vote on the European project.

In the early years of the 21st century, Britain has a wonderful opportunity to embark on a new course that will enable our country to rise to the new challenges that face our world. Our future best lies in becoming a low tax, high enterprise, well educated and vigorously independent nation with a proud heritage and confident forward-looking approach. The EU is not going to help us in this quest; indeed it has become a millstone round our neck and will hold us back until we have the courage to break free.

Foreword
by Lord Stoddart of Swindon

Lord Stoddart was Labour MP for Swindon from 1970.

In 1983 he was raised to the peerage and now sits as Independent Labour. He is joint President of the Campaign for an Independent Britain with Sir Richard Body.

There is mounting concern about the direction being taken by the European Union and its insatiable appetite for accruing to itself further and greater powers at the expense of the member states. The Union has come a long way since the United Kingdom joined the then European Economic Community (Common Market) in 1973. Indeed, it has become the sort of entity predicted by those who opposed joining the EEC, of whom I was one. In fact what is now the European Union has accrued to itself even more powers than was dreamt of by those opponents.

There is now virtually no area of policy from which the EU is excluded. It has competence in matters of trade, justice and the law, health, education, security and law enforcement, the environment, transport, employment, including working hours, defence, foreign affairs, economic and monetary policy as well as areas of taxation. The list is not exhaustive and, even as I write, the President of the Council and the Commission are calling for "economic governance" from Brussels and the European Parliament is calling for the Union to have powers of direct taxation.

As this CIB booklet points out, these powers have been obtained by stealth over a long period of time with the connivance of successive governments and endorsed by supine Westminster Parliaments. A succession of governments have sought to justify the sacrifice of so much of Britain's independence and the payment of huge sums of money into the EU every year (£7billion net this year rising to £10billion in 2012/13) by boasting that 40% of our trade is with The European Union. However, 60% is with countries outside Europe, but Britain is not required to sacrifice much of her independence or pay a large fee for trading with them.

In the title of this booklet the question is asked, "Can Parliament serve two masters: the nation and the European Union?" It clearly cannot do so because many of the policies pursued by the EU are inimical to Britain's best interests, especially in the area of trade and economic development where inappropriate and, sometimes, ridiculous regulations impose large additional costs on British business and enterprise. Furthermore, as is pointed out, the 1972 European Communities Act provides that European law is superior to British law and must be applied in the United Kingdom without further enactment, so Parliament at Westminster cannot refuse to implement Brussels law or hold the Brussels government to account.

The contribution by Anthony Coughlan on the Treaty of Lisbon is worthy of close study for it sets out briefly and in simple language the leap-forward towards full political and economic union that the treaty brings about. In other words the necessary building blocks to full statehood are in place.

Of course there are still those who continue to argue that the Lisbon Treaty is just a clearing-up operation and that there is no ambition to create a single European state, "a country called Europe".

However, the European Union has a President of the Council (Cabinet), a civil service (the Commission), a parliament (the European Parliament), a supreme court (The European Court of Justice), a legal personality (enabling the Union to make treaties in its own right), a foreign secretary (High Representative for Foreign Affairs), an army council, a central bank and a European currency (the euro), a citizenship and citizens of its own, a flag (12 yellow stars on a blue background), an anthem (Beethoven's *Ode to Joy*) and a non-voting seat as of right in the councils of the United Nations (only recently acquired).

The EU, therefore, has all the elements of a fully fledged state and it certainly behaves like one in the area of the Union and throughout the rest of the world. Its global influence will be greatly enhanced by the large diplomatic service now being put in place and the influence of the member states, including the United Kingdom will, in consequence, be reduced.

The Campaign for an Independent Britain believes that it is vital for parliamentarians to understand the real nature of the European Union and its ambitions, for it is only they who can call time on the march to "a country called Europe". There is now a new parliament and a different sort of government from that which we have been used to over the past sixty five years in that it is a coalition of two political parties.

Because it is a coalition the Government cannot simply railroad matters through the House of Commons on whipped votes and restricted discussion. Here, then, is an opportunity for Parliament to assert itself and refuse to cede any further powers to the European Union and, indeed, to demand the return of powers already lost. If Parliament will do this they will regain the support, respect and confidence of the British people, who believe that it is Parliament at Westminster which should govern them and not the undemocratic bureaucracy in Brussels.

THE GRAND DESIGN

Design for Europe 1947
"No government dependent on a democractic vote could possibly agree in advance to the sacrifice that any adequate plan must involve. The British people must be led slowly and unconsciously into the abandonment of their traditional economic defences..."

Peter Thorneycroft, later Chancellor of the Exchequer and Chairman of the Conservative Party.

The European Union started life as the European Coal and Steel Community in the early Fifties, then became the European Economic Community by the Treaty of Rome between the original six member states in 1957. It metamorphosed into the European Community and finally the European Union.

What Germany means by "Integration":
"Does free Europe want to join Germany? Germany is the heart of Europe and the limbs must adjust themselves to the heart, not the heart to the limbs."

HANS SEEBOHM Minister of Commerce in Dr. Adenauer's Government 1950.

Various treaties were landmarks along the way but the process is open ended as the institutions press towards "an ever closer union" between the member nations, as is the stated objective in the Treaty of Rome. There is no doubt that the founders of this remarkable institution saw the creation of a United States of Europe as the aim of this process. The member states would gradually and imperceptibly become as subordinate to Brussels as New York, Rhode Island and California are to Washington.

From The Schumann Declaration

The pooling of coal and steel production should immediately provide for the setting up of common foundations for economic development as a first step in the federation of Europe... a true foundation for their economic unification... By pooling basic production and by instituting a new High Authority, whose decisions will bind France, Germany and other member countries, this proposal will lead to the realization of the first concrete foundation of a European federation indispensable to the preservation of peace.

Robert Schuman, French Foreign Minister, 9th May 1950

British politicians have tended to be rather coy about this objective, presenting the EU as if it were an association of freely cooperating sovereign states with a limited set of objectives, such as free trade between its members. In Britain for many years the European Economic Community was called "The Common Market", giving rise to a not unreasonable popular perception that free trade between members was its sole or main objective – but free trade and all other EU projects were and always are instruments towards achieving closer political union.

"In this challenging time we are naturally encountering difficulties. **They are the birth pangs attending the creation of a United States of Europe**".

Jean Monnet, who has been called "The Father of Europe" April 30 1952, addressingthe Washington Press Club on the European Coal and Steel Community and was being quite open and frank.

The only time that the British people had a say in the matter was in the referendum of 1975. The leaflet issued by HM Government recommending a

"Yes" vote repeatedly used the expressions "Common Market" or "the market", downplaying other aspects of membership with the assurance that Britain would have a permanent veto on any further extensions of EU authority. The Wilson government incorrectly claimed that it had achieved a "fundamental renegotiation" of Britain's terms of membership and that the project for Economic and Monetary Union (basically the euro currency) had been permanently abandoned. With these assurances and a very professional campaign by the European Movement (which was heavily funded by the American Central Intelligence Agency), the British people voted to stay in "The Common Market" by a large majority.

"I was absolutely astonished to discover that the library of Georgetown University, Washington, had the entire archive of a CIA front organisation which documents from start to finish funnelling millions of dollars into Europe and Britain... The whole accounting structure of the European Movement was designed to hide the fact that CIA money was coming in."

Dr Richard Aldridge (Political historian), BBC Radio 4, 3rd Feb 2000,
"Document: a letter to The Times"

Parliament Manipulated (1971/72)

As Prime Minister, Edward Heath promised to take the UK into the European Economic Community only "with the full hearted consent of the British people". In the event, the Commons vote was only 309 to 301 in favour – hardly full hearted, even amongst MPs. This vote was only achieved by a series of very questionable manipulations of procedure. Parliament, in effect, signed a blank cheque on the country's account without knowing the terms of the treaty. Two Labour MPs who were present recount these events on video. They are Nigel Spearing and Eric Deakins. They are interviewed separately in the first two videos and together in the last of the three below. This is a valuable historical record, now available world-wide.

MP Nigel Spearing: *Common Market British Duped*
http://www.blip.tv/file/2330562/
MP Eric Deakins: *Common Market - How The British Were Duped*
http://www.blip.tv/file/2330697/

Common Market - British People Were Duped
http://www.blip.tv/file/2330786/

If you have any difficulty connecting with the website addresses, simply type in the phrase "Common Market British people were duped" to your search engine.

The People Deceived (from 1970 until today)

The following quotations show that Mr Heath was extremely deceitful with the people when describing the European project to them.

1970 "There will be no blueprint for a federal Europe".

1971 "There is no question of any erosion of essential national sovereignty"

"There are some in this country who fear that, in going into Europe, we shall in some way sacrifice independence and sovereignty. These fears, I need hardly say, are completely unjustified".

1975 "There is no danger of a single currency"

1 November 1991 in interview with Peter Sissons:

Sissons "The single currency, the United States of Europe: was that on your mind when you took Britain in?"
Heath "Of course, yes".

All subsequent Prime Ministers have continued in this tradition.

Since then, the EU has expanded and changed dramatically, bringing in nations from former Iron Curtain countries. Expansion of EU competences over different areas of national life has also increased by leaps and bounds.

With a larger number of member states, the need for achieving unanimity was steadily replaced by a system of voting which is weighted according to the populations of the member states. So the interest of any member state can be overruled by a sufficient majority of other countries. As

Britain's pattern of trade and legal system are different from those of mainland members, this has frequently led to disadvantage.

The British government does have influence on new EU proposals through its membership of COREPER, the Committee of Permanent Representatives of member states to the EU Commission. The Commission is a permanent, unelected body with the sole power of initiative in proposing measures to the European Council and EU parliament. Both these bodies can refuse a Commission proposal but they are usually agreed by a process of negotiation and amendments in committee.

Three Little Words

The essence of Britain's relationship with the EU is contained in the European Communities Act of 1972 which outsources much of our lawmaking to the EU institutions and states that these and all future EU laws become binding on Britain in their entirety **"without further enactment"**. Whilst that clause remains in force, Parliament has little or no say in those laws which the EU chooses to impose on us.

Generally speaking, EU laws arrive in two main ways:

REGULATIONS – made by the European Council upon a proposal by the Commission with the agreement of the EU parliament. Once enacted by the council of heads of government or relevant ministers with the requisite majority, these become immediately binding throughout the EU without any input from Parliament.

DIRECTIVES – These are instructions by the EU, arrived at much as above, but requiring the national parliaments of member states to enact them into law on their own statute books. Members of Parliament are frequently unaware that Bills or clauses introduced by government are the result of such Directives. Brussels is the puppet master, the British government is the string and Parliament and MPs are the marionettes.

There are other extra-parliamentary sources of law, such as areas of authority delegated to the EU Commission by the institutions and judgements of the European Court of Justice (ECJ).

For the whole of its existence, the European Court of Justice has taken an activist view of its function rather than one merely interpretative of the body of European law (*Aquis Communautaire*). It too sees its job as hastening the process of "ever closer union". So, in some ways, it behaves more like an unelected legislature rather than the way in which a British court would operate.

The British government has been very reluctant to admit how much of its legislative programme is dictated by the EU. A written question in the German Parliament produced an answer that over 80 per cent of laws being passed to govern the German people arose from EU institutions and obligations. As the German constitution states that "all authority emanates from the (German) people", this produced some interesting debate. The accumulated weight of regulations, directives and judgements on all EU countries is now enormous.

"Like an invisible hand, the EU operates through existing political structures. There are no European courts, legislatures or business regulations on display in London. The British House of Commons, British law courts and British civil servants are still there but they uphold and implement European law. By creating common standards that are implemented through national institutions, Europe can envelope countries without becoming a target for hostility…"

March 2005 **Mark Leonard**, *a Europhile, in "How the EU deceives its way to power":*

Because EU legislation is not clearly identified in the statute book or fully understood, Members of Parliament and even government ministers are frequently unaware of how limited their freedom of action has become. To give one example: the Conservative government introduced VAT on domestic fuel, gas and electricity. The then Labour opposition made a commitment to repeal this tax which, they felt, was an undue burden on people with low incomes. When Labour came to power, they were unable to deliver their promise. Once an area of life has become an EU "competence" it can never be taken back by a member state. By urgent application to the EU authorities, they were given permission to reduce the tax from 7.5% to 5% but they could not keep their promise and repeal it. So this is one area in which Parliament has actually lost its basic power over taxation. There are many more similar situations where powers have been transferred and MPs have remained unaware or have been unwilling to defend the rights of their House.

Civil Liberties and Law

The EU aspires to be "a common area of freedom and justice" and to establish a single, legal code throughout its territory. As all the other EU states apart from Ireland have Roman law systems, it is clear that the British Common Law system will eventually be abolished by this process. A typical episode in this process occurred in 1999. The EU parliament voted to accept a legal code called "Corpus Juris" (Body of Law). This provided for a European Public Prosecutor with the right to arrest people without charge and take them anywhere within the EU.

The Prosecutor can keep people locked up in "investigative custody" for an infinitely renewable sequence of 12 week periods, subject to review by an official with the rather Orwellian title "Judge of Freedoms". The accused does not have to appear in open court, so Habeas Corpus is abolished. If the Prosecutor does bring someone to trial there will be no jury. If the accused is found not guilty, the Prosecutor can appeal against acquittal. There is no rule against double jeopardy.

Both the Labour government and Conservative opposition were resolutely opposed to this proposal. Nonetheless both Labour and Conservative MEPs voted FOR it! Most votes in the EU parliament are taken in sessions where hundreds of items an hour are voted through and MEPs have no idea what they are voting for, unless it something in which they have taken a personal interest. They simply vote to a "shopping list" prepared by their EU parliamentary group. That is the extent of democratic scrutiny in the EU. The defects and unfairnesses of the EU arrest warrant procedures have become apparent of recent years.

Even the EU Commission has noticed that some EU jurisdictions are notably corrupt. Yet a judge or prosecutor in these states can issue an arrest warrant for anyone in Britain. All the British court is allowed to do is (a) to check that the warrant has been issued by a genuine official (b) that the person named on the warrant is the one they have before them and (c) that the offence is one carrying a sentence of a year's imprisonment or more. No *prima facie* evidence is needed and the offence does not need to be an offence under British law nor committed on the territory of the state making the accusation. The Lisbon Treaty contains provision for the European Public Prosecutor. Whilst the British government has an opt out for the time being from accepting his authority, it is not obligated to consult Parliament before changing its mind.

Disuniting the Kingdom

"The transfer of major executive responsibilities to the bureaucratic Commission in Brussels will exacerbate popular feelings of alienation from government. To counter this feeling, strengthened local and regional democratic processes within member states and effective Community economic and social policies will be essential... there would be a major responsibility on HM Government and on all political parties not to exacerbate public concern by attributing unpopular policies to the remote and unmanageable workings of the Community."

Foreign Office document of 1971, ref: FCO 30/1048 (1971).

English regions and devolution in Scotland, Wales and Northern Ireland were set up by British legislation to comply with EU requirements. EU discretionary grants are awarded at regional level, bypassing central government. Scotland Wales and Northern Ireland are EU regions. The English regions were set up arbitrarily to meet the EU requirement, having no prior identity or real internal cohesion. The regions compete against each other for EU grants and have "mini embassies" in Brussels to plead their case. Clearly, those regions showing the greatest commitment to EU objectives will be the most favoured. This is part of a divide-and-rule strategy which is being followed all over the EU to weaken nation states and create "perforated sovereignty" within them. In Britain's case it is peculiarly disadvantageous because all we get is the return of a proportion of our own money to spend on priorities approved by the EU. The devolution of agricultural, NHS and other policies means that we have, in effect, four differently administered policies within the UK. This sort of thing is unnecessarily and deliberately divisive. It can only have been intentionally designed to stir up ill feeling between the peoples of the UK. The break up of the United Kingdom has been the aim of every major continental power since it was established in 1707. As long as Brussels controls and influences the process through the Committee of the Regions, the structures will be a sham and a danger.

The objectives of this policy, taken with other EU measures, were expressed quite clearly by Giuliano Amato, a former Italian Prime Minister and more recently Vice President of the European Constitutional Convention.

"[Amato] said that however daring a political project might be... it must be hidden, camouflaged. One must act 'as if' in Europe. 'As if' one wanted a very few things in order to obtain a great deal. 'As if' nations were to remain sovereign in order to convince them to surrender their sovereignty. The Commission in Brussels, for example, must act 'as if' it were a technical organ in order to operate like a government.

He said that sovereignty lost on a national level does not pass to any new individual. It is entrusted to a faceless entity... eventually the EU. The [European] Union is the vanguard of this changing world... The new entity is faceless and those in command can neither be identified nor elected. As a matter of fact the metamorphosis is already here. All we need are a few corrections here and there along with a great deal of cunning..."

from an article in La Stampa of 13 July 2000 in an interview with Barbara Spinelli, headed, "Europe does not need a sovereign"

It is clear that the slogan "Independence in Europe" is as meaningless and deceitful as was "In Europe but not run by Europe".

Whilst the coalition Government has announced the disbandment of much of the present English regional structures, it has not made clear what institutions will be established to meet the unaltered treaty obligations.

Freedom of speech and the Press

The unelected EU Commission has signalled its intent to control all press and media by issuing an EU Press Card. They will decide who can and cannot be a journalist. A 16 page document has already been issued, telling the EU press corps how it should and should not report the EU. Following an angry response from the journalists this was quickly withdrawn – but only from the public domain. It is waiting its turn to be reintroduced.

This may initially be on a 'voluntary' basis but its power will be steadily strengthened over time until it could well become impossible to operate as a journalist without an EU press card. The Commission also aspires to control the Internet, websites and blogging.

"Criticism of the EU is akin to blasphemy and can be restricted without affecting freedom of speech."

Ruiz Jarabo Colomer, Advocate General of the EU Court of Justice, gave this opinion on 19th October 2000 (Case c-274/99)

The Court of First Instance has previously ruled that "the EU may restrict political speech to protect its interests."

The Democratic Deficit

The EU Constitution was democratically rejected by the peoples of France and the Netherlands. It was also rejected by the German Constitutional Court because it contravened the principle in the German constitution that "all authority emanates from the people". The Lisbon treaty achieved almost identical transfers of powers to the EU institutions by different methods. This is a good time to look at what it actually does so that legislators and citizens may be aware of the provisions, concealed in its deliberately opaque language. It certainly marks a major step along the road to that "ever closer union" of European nations and the inevitable consequent reduction of democratic safeguards, previously thought to be within the undoubted power of a Parliament deriving it authority from consent of the governed which, in the case of Lisbon, was never sought.

Anthony Coughlan is President of the
Foundation for EU Democracy, Brussels,
Belgium, and Director of the National
Platform EU Research and Information Centre,
Dublin, Ireland;
He is Senior Lecturer Emeritus in Social
Policy, Trinity College, Dublin.

Website: nationalplatform.org
Phone 00-353-1-8305792

THE TREATY OF LISBON: A CONSTITUTIONAL REVOLUTION BY STEALTH

With the coming into force of the Lisbon Treaty on 1 December 2009, members of the European Parliament, who previously had been "representatives of the peoples of the States brought together in the Community" (Art.189 TEC), became "representatives of the Union's citizens" (Art.14 TEU).

This change in the legal status of MEPs is but one illustration of the constitutional revolution being brought about by the Lisbon Treaty.

For Lisbon, like the EU Constitution before it, establishes for the first time a European Union which is constitutionally separate from and superior to its Member States, just as the USA is separate from and superior to its 50 constituent states, or as Federal Germany is in relation to its Länder.

The 27 EU members thereby lose their character as true sovereign States. Constitutionally, they become more like regional states in a multinational Federation, although they still retain some of the trappings of their former sovereignty. Simultaneously, 500 million Europeans become real citizens of the constitutionally new post-Lisbon European Union, with real citizens' rights and duties with regard to this EU, as compared with the merely notional or symbolical EU citizenship they are assumed to have possessed up to now.

Most Europeans are unaware of these astonishing changes, for two reasons. One is that, with the exception of the Irish, they have been denied any chance of learning about and debating them in national referendums. The other is that the terms "European Union", "EU citizen" and "EU citizenship" remain the same before and after Lisbon, although Lisbon changes their constitutional content fundamentally.

The Lisbon Treaty therefore is a constitutional revolution by stealth.

A constitutionally new European Union

Lisbon's predecessor, The Treaty Establishing a Constitution for Europe, which the peoples of France and Holland rejected in referendums in 2005, sought to establish a new European Union in the constitutional form of a Federation directly. Its first article stated: "This Constitution establishes the European Union". That would clearly have been a European Union with a different constitutional basis from the EU that had been set up by the Maastricht Treaty 13 years before.

Lisbon brings a constitutionally new Union into being indirectly rather than directly, by amending the two existing European Treaties instead of replacing them entirely, as the earlier Constitutional Treaty had sought to do. Thus Lisbon states: "The Union shall be founded on the present Treaty" - viz. the Treaty on European Union (TEU) - "and on the Treaty on the Functioning of the Union." These two Treaties together then become the Constitution of the post-Lisbon European Union. A legally new Union is in effect being "constituted", although the word "Constitution" is not used.

What we called the "European Union" pre-Lisbon is the descriptive term for the totality of legal relations between its 27 Member States and their peoples. This encompassed the European Community, which had legal personality, made supranational European laws and had various State-like features, as well as the Member States cooperating together on the basis of retained sovereignty in foreign policy and defence and in crime and justice matters.

Lisbon changes this situation fundamentally by giving the post-Lisbon Union the constitutional form of a true supranational Federation, in other words a State. The EU would still lack some powers of a fully developed

Federation, the most obvious one being the power to force its Member States to go to war against their will. It would possess most of the powers of a State however, although it has nothing like the actual tax and spending levels of its constituent Member States.

Three steps to a federal-style Constitution

Lisbon's constitutional revolution takes place in three interconnected steps:

Firstly, the Treaty establishes a European Union with legal personality and a fully independent corporate existence in all Union areas for the first time (Arts.1 and 47 TEU). This enables the post-Lisbon Union to function as a State *vis-à-vis* other States externally, and in relation to its own citizens internally.

Secondly, Lisbon abolishes the European Community which goes back to the Treaty of Rome and which makes European laws at present, and transfers the Community's powers and institutions to the new Union, so that it is the post-Lisbon Union, not the Community, which will make supranational European laws henceforth (Art.1 TEU). Lisbon also transfers to the EU the "intergovernmental" powers over crime, justice and home affairs, as well as foreign policy and security, which at present are not covered by European law-making, leaving only aspects of the Common Foreign, Security and Defence Policy outside the scope of its supranational powers. The Treaty thereby give a unified constitutional structure to the post-Lisbon Union.

Thirdly, Lisbon then makes 500 million Europeans into real citizens of the new Federal-style Union which the Treaty establishes (Arts.9 TEU and 20 TFEU). Instead of EU citizenship "complementing" national citizenship, as under the present Maastricht Treaty-based EU (Art.17 TEC) - which makes such citizenship essentially symbolical - Lisbon provides that EU citizenship shall be "additional to" national citizenship.

This is a real dual citizenship - not of two different States, but of two different levels of one State. One can only be a citizen of a State and all States must have citizens. Dual citizenship like that provided for in Lisbon is normal in classical Federations which have been established from the bottom up by constituent states surrendering their sovereignty to a superior federal entity, in contrast to federations that have come into being "top-down", as it were, as a result of unitary states adopting federal form. Examples of the former are the

USA, 19th Century Germany, Switzerland, Canada, Australia. Lisbon would confer a threefold citizenship on citizens of Federal Germany's Länder.

Being a citizen means that one must obey the law and give loyalty to the authority of the State one is a citizen of - in the case of classical Federations, of the two state levels, the federal and the regional or provincial. In the post-Lisbon EU the rights and duties attaching to citizenship of the Union will be superior to those attaching to one's national citizenship in any case of conflict between the two, because of the superiority of Union law over national law and Constitutions (Declaration No 17 concerning Primacy).

The EU will be constitutionally superior even though the powers of the new Union come from its Member States in accordance with the "principle of conferral" (Art.5 TEU). Where else after all could it get its powers from? This is so even though the Member States retain their national Constitutions and their citizens keep their national citizenships. The local states of the USA retain their different state Constitutions and citizenships to this day, even though both are subordinate to the US Federal Constitution in any case of conflict between the two. The tenth amendment to the US Constitution embodies the principle of conferral when it lays down that powers not delegated to the US Federation "are reserved to the states respectively, or to the people".

Likewise, it is not unusual for the Constitutions of classical Federations to provide for a right of withdrawal for their constituent states, just as the Lisbon Treaty does (Art.50 TEU). Joseph Stalin's constitution of the former USSR incorporated this principle. The existence of these features in the Constitution of the post-Lisbon Union does not take away from its federalist character.

An alternative source of democratic legitimacy to the Nation State

Under Lisbon population size will in turn become the primary basis for EU law-making, as in any State with a common citizenry. This will happen after 2014, when the Treaty provision comes into force that EU laws will be made by 55% of the Member States - currently 15 out of 25 - as long as they represent between them 65% of the total population of the Union. Germany and France together have one-third of the EU's population.

Lisbon provides an alternative source of democratic legitimacy which challenges the right of national governments to be the representatives of their electorates in the EU. The amended Treaty provides: "The functioning of the Union shall be founded on representative democracy. Citizens are directly represented at Union level in the European Parliament. Member States are represented in the European Council by their Heads of State or Government and in the Council by their governments" (Art.10 TEU). Contrast this with what is stated to be the foundation of the present Maastricht Treaty-based EU: "The Union is founded on the principles of liberty, democracy, respect for human rights and fundamental freedoms, and the rule of law, principles which are common to the Member States" (Art.6 TEU).

The constitutional structure of the post-Lisbon EU is completed by the provision which turns the European Council of Prime Ministers and Presidents into an "institution" of the new Union (Art.13 TEU), so that its acts, or its failing to act would, like those of the other Union institutions, be subject to legal review by the EU Court of Justice.

Constitutionally speaking, the summit meetings of the European Council will henceforth no longer be "intergovernmental" gatherings outside supranational European structures, as they have been up to now. The European Council will in effect be the Cabinet Government of the post-Lisbon Union. Its individual members will be constitutionally obliged to represent the Union to their Member States as well as their Member States to the Union, with the former function imposing primacy of legal obligation in any case of conflict or tension between the two.

One doubts if all the Heads of State or Government who make up the European Council themselves appreciate this! Nor is it constitutionally valid to regard relations between the Member States of the post-Lisbon Union as "foreign" relations any longer. Some Foreign Ministers were upset that they were not invited to take part in the first post-Lisbon meeting of the European Council in December 2009, for in pre-Lisbon days Foreign Ministers and their officials took for granted that they attended these quarterly "summit" meetings at which their Prime Ministers or Presidents were representing their Member States outside Union constitutional structures.

As regards the State authority of the post-Lisbon Union, this will be embodied in the Union's own legislative, executive and judicial institutions:

the European Council, Council of Ministers, Parliament, Commission and Court of Justice. It will be embodied also in the Member States and their authorities as they implement and apply EU law and interpret and apply national law in conformity with Union law. Member States will be constitutionally required to do this under the Lisbon Treaty. Thus EU "State authorities" as represented for example by EU soldiers and policemen patrolling our streets in EU uniforms, will not be needed as such.

Although the Lisbon Treaty has given the EU a Federal-style Constitution without most people noticing, they are bound to find out in time and react against what is being done. There is no European people or demos which could give democratic legitimacy to the institutions the Lisbon Treaty establishes and make people identify with these as they do with the institutions of their home countries. This is the core problem of the EU integration project. Lisbon in effect has made the EU's democratic deficit much worse.

It is hard to imagine that this will not make struggles to re-establish national independence and democracy and to repatriate supranational powers back to the Member States the central issue of European politics in the years and decades ahead.

Anthony Coughlan

A Plea to MPs and Peers

Parliament is held in very low esteem. This is unhealthy for such democracy as still remains outside the EU's competence. The modest beginnings of the elaborate system of perks and expenses, which caused such scandal recently, occurred in 1971 when negotiations preceding the European Communities Act 1972 were at their most intense. As Parliament began to outsource huge swathes of its lawmaking responsibilities, so pay, pensions, staff and conditions for MPs were, by stages, made hugely more generous.

It is surely reasonable to expect today's MPs and Peers to inform themselves fully of those laws which they are compelled to enact by EU requirements and to acquaint themselves with the limits of what Parliament can do as a provincial EU Assembly, albeit one with a bit of pageantry attached. There surely must be a duty to be precise and frank with constituents and petitioners who are caught in the toils of bureaucracy, which Parliament has allowed to slip from its control.

Much is made today of the need for "transparency" but there has been very little of it with regard to the superior power of the EU over the laws and lives of British people. Even highly eurosceptic newspapers often still refer to "new government initiatives" when a little basic research would show that the initiatives come from Brussels not Downing Street.

"Not only was it wrong for us to deal superficially with what Europe involved, but we've paid the price for it ever since, because every time there's a crisis in Europe, people say, with some justification, 'Well we would not have been part of this if we'd really known the implications.'"

Notable europhile, Lord Hattersley, BBC Radio 4, 3rd February 2000

That, we believe, is the reason why Britain never has been and never will be at ease with itself in an institution so profoundly alien to the British way of doing things. A reasonable, friendly and cooperative relationship with our European neighbours is perfectly possible outside the political institutions of the European Union. Trade would not be affected. Many countries have access to the EU single market without being subject to political structures.

The Campaign for an Independent Britain (CIB) is a non-party organisation, drawing support from across the mainstream of political opinion and from people independent of party. We invite like-minded parliamentarians to join us in regaining the honour of their Houses and the trust of the people they serve.